Happy Thanksgiving, Betty!

Love, Bev

Enjoy Reading

11-17-08

This Book Belongs to:

_____

Tommy NELSON

Off to Plymouth Rock!

By **Dandi Daley Mackall**

Illustrations by **Gene Barretta**

Tommy NELSON

www.tommynelson.com

A Division of Thomas Nelson, Inc.
www.ThomasNelson.com

Published in Nashville, Tennessee, by Tommy Nelson®, a Division of Thomas Nelson, Inc.

Library of Congress Cataloging-in-Publication Data

Mackall, Dandi Daley.

    Off to Plymouth Rock! / by Dandi Daley Mackall.

      p. cm.

    Summary: Easy, rhyming text describes the voyage of the Pilgrims, their work in building a new home in America, and their celebration held in thanksgiving for a rich harvest.

    ISBN 1-4003-0194-7 (hardcover)

    ISBN 1-4003-0473-3 (hardcover w/CD)

    1. Pilgrims (New Plymouth Colony)--Juvenile literature. 2. Thanksgiving Day--History--Juvenile literature. 3. Massachusetts--History--New Plymouth, 1620-1691--Juvenile literature. [1. Pilgrims (New Plymouth Colony) 2. Thanksgiving Day--History. 3. Massachusetts--History--New Plymouth, 1620-1691.] I. Title.

F68.M143 2003

394.2649--dc21

                               2003004646

Printed in the United States of America
05 06 07 08 LBM 5 4 3 2
06 07 08 LBM 5 4

Dedication

Since this is a Thanksgiving book, I'd like to give thanks to God for all the wonderful people he has surrounded me with:

- My amazing husband, Joe—best writer, editor, friend, and husband a girl ever had.
- Daughter Jen—great daughter, great friend, talented writer and historian.
- Daughter Katy—great daughter, with a sweet, sweet spirit, and special way with animals.
- Son Dan—great son, with a good heart and a terrific sense of humor.
- My mom, Helen Eberhart Daley, who taught me most of what I know about hard work.
- My dad, who passed down his creativity and ever-active mind. I miss you and know you're watching.
- My sister, Maureen Pento—best big sis a little sis ever had . . . and the whole Pento clan: Tom, Chris & Rebecca, Kelly & Billy Bob.
- My in-laws—Jim and Peg Mackall and all the Mackalls and McCarthys who welcomed me into their world.
- My buddy, Laurie Knowlton . . . and all the terrific friends who keep me going.
- And thanks to my editor, who said, "Dandi, we have a whole page for your dedication. Go ahead and write an Oscar speech."

For my mom, who lives on the tip of my paintbrush and
dances in God's garden.
I love you.
—G

Pilgrims flee!
Sail the sea,
Knowing there's no guarantee.

Leaving, grieving,
Still believing . . .
Off to Plymouth Rock!

Mayflower ship—
    Dangerous trip!
Waves that rock and winds that whip.

Crashing, splashing,
    Lightning flashing!
On to Plymouth Rock!

Land ahoy!
     Shouts of joy!
Cheers from every girl and boy.

Steering, veering,
     There's a clearing!
On to Plymouth Rock!

Sawing beams—
Work in teams—
Building up their Pilgrim dreams.

Blizzards pounding,
   Snows abounding—
Here at Plymouth Rock!

Massasoit,
Indian king,
Sees the Pilgrims suffering.

Shivering, praying,
Still they're staying
Here at Plymouth Rock!

Watchful Squanto
    Understands,
  Shares the secrets of the lands.

Digging, hoeing,
   Corn is growing—
Here at Plymouth Rock!

Pilgrims call
    One and all,
Come and celebrate the fall!

Pumpkins, cherries,
    Turkey, berries,
Here at Plymouth Rock!

Glad to share—
Bow in prayer—
Harvest blessings everywhere.

Humble living,
    First Thanksgiving—
Here at Plymouth Rock!